What industry professionals are saying about
Quick! The Cement Is Drying:

Jim Zara, CLU, ChFC, 14-year agent, lifetime Million Dollar Round Table, Top of the Table producer

Every agency manager in the financial services world would be wise to give "Quick! The Cement Is Drying" to all of their new agents and to anyone else in the recruiting process who is seriously thinking about a career in this industry. This terrific book should also be required reading for any veteran agent who has been on a plateau for more than a year.

Jeff Tyler, CLU, ChFC, Managing Partner

Proverbs states that "words appropriately spoken are like golden oranges on trays of silver. They are refreshing, strengthening, pleasing and uplifting." This book captures the wisdom of Solomon for the new financial representative and helps equip them to enjoy meaningful and fulfilling careers in financial services.

Scott Dudley, Field Director

Of all the recommended books on motivation and success, "Quick! The Cement Is Drying" by Sabine Robinson is one of the single best sources on how to successfully build a career in the financial services and insurance industry. Anyone considering a career in this field must read Sabine's book. It is a window into the opportunities and challenges that all new agents will face.

Kara Short, new agent coach

Every person considering a career in financial services or coaching new agents should read this book. Sabine paints a clear picture of the emotional ups and downs of this unique sales career. Each "bit of wisdom" has a different meaning to agents at different stages of the business. It is definitely a book that should be read again and again through both trying and exciting times. I spend months conveying this information to the agents I coach. Here it is, condensed in one place.

Noah N. Farnham, M.B.A., first-year agent

I loved the book! "Quick! The Cement Is Drying" is a wonderful and positive book that should be a resource for every new financial professional. It contains everything someone new in the business needs to know to help ensure a fast start. There is an uplifting and positive message regarding almost every type of problem that is encountered. Sabine gives outstanding advice on how to establish good habits from the very beginning of your career.

Jamie Weber, three-year agent

"Quick! The Cement Is Drying" is fantastic! Sabine conveys nearly every emotion and thought that a new agent will have early in his or her career. If you truly believe what she writes and embrace it, you will build a lasting career with all the right habits. Having this book handy is the next best thing to having Sabine coach you in person.

Marcia Niekamp, CLU, ChFC, five-year agent

"Quick! The Cement Is Drying" is a must-read for all agents in the financial services industry. This book would also be extremely helpful for those even considering a career in this field. Sabine's creative and insightful collection of wisdom contains everything an agent needs in his or her arsenal to build a successful practice. This is the only book I know of written specifically for our industry.